Animals of the Night

OWLS AFTER DARK

Ruth O'Shaughnessy

Enslow Publishing
101 W. 23rd Street
Suite 240
New York, NY 10011
USA

enslow.com

Words to Know

binocular vision—The ability to focus both eyes on an object at once.

burrow—A tunnel or hole in the ground used by an animal.

camouflage—The use of an animal's coloring to blend in with its surroundings.

mate—The process through which animals have young. A mate can also be the female or male partner of an animal.

nocturnal—Active at night.

predator—An animal that kills other animals for food.

prey—An animal that is hunted for food.

raptor—A bird with strong legs, powerful feet, and sharp claws.

species—A type of animal.

talons—Razor-sharp claws.

Contents

After Sundown

In the quiet twilight, most creatures are falling asleep. But one creature is wide awake and hungry: the owl that lives in a tree in the park. He turns his head this way and that, searching for food.

Finally, the bird spreads its wings and flies through an open space, into the night air. Easily flying through the trees, the owl swoops down, reaching at the ground with its sharp talons. Its prey, a small mouse, is carried into the nearest tree.

This owl, like most others, is active during the nighttime hours. That is why they are seen less often than other birds. But it's almost certain you've heard one before: "whoo-whoo-whoo-whoo."

A little owl flies in the night,
hunting for prey.

Birds of a Feather

There are over two-hundred species of owl, living in different habitats all over the world. They are all different sizes too. A great gray owl can grow as tall as 33 inches (84 centimeters). From tip to tip, its wings measure about 5 feet (1½ meters) across, about the length of a bathtub.

The smallest owl, the elf owl, grows no more than 5 to 6 inches (13 to 15 centimeters) tall. That is just a little shorter than a new pencil. There are lots of other owls in between these. Some weigh as little as 1½ ounces (42½ grams) and others as much as 9 pounds (4 kilograms). The great horned owl is a large, heavy owl. Barn owls are medium-sized owls. The Northern Saw-whet owl has a small body with a large head.

The elf owl is the smallest species of owl.

Owls have eyes in the front of their heads, just like humans do. Unlike humans, owls' eyes do not move around in the socket. Instead, owls turn their whole heads to see.

Different owls have different calls. Not all sound like they are saying "whoo" or "hoot." Some owls make a barking sound. Others hiss, whistle, snort, or screech. The barred owl's call sounds like "Who cooks for you?"

Fun Fact!

Owls can't turn their heads completely around. They can go about three-quarters of a circle. That is still a lot farther around than what people can do, which is about half a circle.

An owl's eyes are in the front of its head. This helps it spot and catch prey while hunting.

Habitats

Owls live in a variety of places—from forests and swamps to deserts and arctic tundra. Many owls even live in cities and suburbs. And although many owls nest in trees, not all owls do. Burrowing owls nest underground. They use the old **burrows** of ground squirrels, prairie dogs, and other small animals.

Most owls tend to stay far away from humans. But barn owls and screech owls sometimes live in barns, church steeples, and other buildings. These owls feed on mice and rats near farms and towns.

Fun Fact!

Owls live on every continent but Antarctica.

This eastern screech owl nests in a tree. Other screech owls may live in buildings.

Nightlife

Most owls are **nocturnal**, meaning that they are most active at night. They have powerful senses that help them survive in the dark. For example, they have very good eyesight even in dim light. Unlike most birds, owls have **binocular vision**. They can focus both eyes on an object at once. This helps them see how near their prey is.

Owls also have excellent hearing. They can hear sounds that people cannot hear. This helps them hunt the animals they eat after dark. An owl can hear a mouse running in the leaves more than 20 yards (18 meters) away.

An eagle owl focuses
its eyes on a rabbit and
prepares to take flight.

Not only do many animals not see owls at night, they also do not hear them. Owls have feathers with soft tips. They do not make the swooshing sound birds with hard-tipped feathers make when they fly. An owl's prey will not hear the owl coming because of its feathers' soft tips.

Fun Fact!

Some owls are crepuscular, meaning they are most active during twilight hours.

The mouse does not hear the owl swooping in for it. The bird's soft-tipped feathers do not make noise.

Hunting

Owls are **raptors**, meaning they are birds that eat other animals. Owls hunt many different prey, from mice, insects, lizards and frogs, to hares, squirrels, snakes, and even other birds. Some types of Asian and African owls eat fish.

All raptors have extremely strong legs and powerful feet. Owls also have razor-sharp claws called talons. The talons are used to grasp and kill prey. Some owls use their large hooked beaks to help with this. Owls also often use their talons to carry their prey through the air.

Fun Fact!

Barn owls are better at catching mice than cats are. A family of barn owls will eat about thirteen hundred mice a year.

Barn owls are excellent mouse catchers.

Owls swallow their small prey whole. They use their beaks and talons to tear up larger prey. These pieces are swallowed without chewing as well. The prey's bones, teeth, claws, and feathers are coughed up in small, hard balls called pellets. Scientists and students sometimes study these pellets to learn more about what owls eat.

Fun Fact!

Scientists have found owl fossils that date back to dinosaur days.

Owl pellets contain the undigested
bones of the animals the owl ate.

Owl Families

Some species of owls stay with one **mate** for life, while others do not. Owls lay their eggs in a nest, but they usually do not build their own nests. Instead, owls often use nests left by other birds.

Most female owls lay between two and six eggs. It takes about fifteen to thirty-five days for the eggs to hatch. The owl chicks are not all born at the same time, but hatch over a period of two days.

A great gray owl cares for her two chicks.

Young owls are blind at birth and have only a thin layer of down, or feathers, to keep them warm. The mother owl feeds her chicks and protects them from **predators**. Father owls bring back food for the family too. At first, the chicks eat insects. As they grow older, they have larger prey.

The parents teach their chicks to fly and hunt. After about two or three months, the young owls are ready to leave the nest.

Fun Fact!

Female owls are usually bigger than males. Some scientists think they are bigger so they can protect the nest. Others believe that females need to catch larger prey than males.

Barn owl chicks huddle together in a pile of hay.

Owl Opponents

Although large adult owls have few predators, smaller owls and chicks have many enemies. They are eaten by larger owls, coyotes, weasels, hawks, raccoons, and other animals. Young owls are especially in danger of being killed. Only about half of them make it to adulthood.

The color of an owl's feathers will often blend in with it habitat. This is called camouflage, and it helps animals hide from predators. Snowy owls are mostly white, which helps keep them invisible in their snowy habitat. Many owls are brown or gray, which helps them to hide in the trees.

A snowy owl blends in with its surroundings.

Relationship with People

Owls and humans often live together in harmony. Humans find owls very helpful since they eat mice and insects that can harm crops. In medieval times, many castles and estates had nest boxes used to encourage owls to live on the property. Many modern properties still have these today.

In many cultures, owls were associated with magic. Owls have symbolized wisdom throughout the world, while some ancient cultures considered them a bad omen. But owls are simply birds trying to live in the wild.

Many owls have become endangered, or at risk of dying out, thanks to humans. They are sometimes poisoned when farm fields are sprayed with chemicals to kill weeds and insects. Hunting owls is against the law in the United States. But these birds are sometimes hunted anyway.

A barred owl perches on a handler's arm at the Center for Wildlife sanctuary in York, Maine.

Endangered and Threatened

There are several species of owl that have become endangered or threatened. This is because owls are losing their habitats. Owls need wide-open spaces and forests to live. But in a lot of areas, such places are disappearing. Many trees have been cut down for timber. Wooded areas are also often cleared to build houses. These areas are also home to the owl's prey. When these areas are gone, owls lose the food they need.

Laws have been passed to protect owls from being hunted or poisoned, and in some places, laws also protect the owl's habitat. With our help, owls can have a better future. It is up to humans to protect them.

A veterinarian examines a barn owl. Many people are working hard to save owls from dying out.

Stay Safe Around Owls

It is in an owl's nature to stay away from people. But as they lose their natural habitats, they may move into cities and towns. Some owls may even make homes in barns and other buildings near farms to hunt the rodents that live there. You are more likely to hear an owl than to see one. But if you live in an area with owls around, it is a good idea to follow some rules to stay safe:

- Never try to keep an owl as a pet. It is illegal in the United States, and they belong in the wild anyway.

- If you come across a live or dead owl, do not touch it. Tell an adult.

- Do not touch owl pellets you may find outside. They can have germs that can make you sick.

- Stay away from owl nests. Mother owls can attack if they think you are a threat to their babies.

- Keep your pets indoors at night. A large owl can attack a cat or small dog. And if you keep rabbits in an outdoor hutch, make sure it can keep them safe from predators.

Learn More

Books

Hoena, Blake. *Everything Birds of Prey*. Des Moines, Iowa: National Geographic Children's Books, 2015.

Kerrod, Robin. *Birds of Prey*. Helotes, Tex.: Armadillo, 2015.

Mara, Wil. *Owls*. New York: Cavendish Square, 2014.

Zeiger, Jennifer. *Snowy Owls*. Danbury, Conn.: Children's Press, 2014.

Web Sites

animals.nationalgeographic.com/animals/birds/snowy-owl/
Read about the snowy owl.

animals.nationalgeographic.com/animals/birds/great-horned-owl/
Learn about the great horned owl.

animals.sandiegozoo.org/animals/owl
Discover fascinating facts about owls.

Index

Published in 2016 by Enslow Publishing, LLC.
101 W. 23rd Street, Suite 240, New York, NY 10011

Copyright © 2016 by the estate of Elaine Landau
Enslow Publishing materials copyright © 2016 by Enslow Publishing, LLC.

Library of Congress Cataloging-in-Publication Data
O'Shaughnessy, Ruth, author.
Owls after dark / Ruth O'Shaughnessy.
    pages cm. — (Animals of the night)
Summary: "Discusses owls, their behavior, and their environment"—Provided blisher.
Audience: ges 8+
Audience: Grades 4 to 6.
Includes bibliographical references and index.
ISBN 978-0-7660-6760-8 (library binding)
ISBN 978-0-7660-6758-5 (pbk.)
ISBN 978-0-7660-6759-2 (6-pack)
1. Owls—Juvenile literature. 2. Nocturnal birds—Juvenile literature.
3. Animal behavior—Juvenile literature. I. Title.
 QL696.S8O84 2016
 598.9'7—dc23
                    2015009972

Printed in the United States of America

To Our Readers: We have done our best to make sure all Web site addresses in this book were active and appropriate when we went to press. However, the author and the publisher have no control over and assume no liability for the material available on those Web sites or on any Web sites they may link to. Any comments or suggestions can be sent by e-mail to customerservice@enslow.com.

Portions of this book originally appeared in the book *Owls: Hunters of the Night.*

Photo Credits: Bill McMullen/Moment/Getty Images (great gray owl), p. 1; Craig K. Lorenz/Science Source/Getty Images, p. 7; Danita Delimont/Gallo Images/Getty Images, p. 25; Dave King/Dorling Kindersley/Getty Images, p. 19; Dennis Green/Oxford Scientific/Getty Images, p. 23; Hein von Horsten/Gallo Images/Getty Images, p. 17; Joseph Van Os/The Image Bank/Getty Images, p. 11; kimberrywood/Digital Vision Vectors/Getty Images (green moon dingbat); Michael Blann/Stone/Getty images, p. 13; Michael Leach/Oxford Scientific/Getty Images, p. 5; m/photos/tango-/5762887776/"ti/Moment/Getty Images, p. 9; narvikk/E+/Getty Images (starry background); Portland Press Herald/Getty images, p. 27; Renaud Visage/Photographer's Choice/Getty Images, p. 15; Rolfe Kopfle/Photo Library/Getty Images, p. 21; Samantha Nicol Art Photography/Moment/Getty Images, p. 3; samxmeg/E+/Getty Images (moon folios and series logo); Visuals Unlimited, Inc/ Gerald Lacz/Getty Images, p. 29.

Cover Credits: Bill McMullen/Moment/Getty Images (great gray owl); narvikk/E+/Getty Images (starry background); kimberrywood/Digital Vision Vectors/Getty Images (green moon dingbat); samxmeg/E+/Getty Images (moon).